Overview *Fred's Doghouse*

Fred tricks Rosie into getting out of bed.

Reading Vocabulary Words

slippers
outside
steps

High-Frequency Words

put	best
where	around
ran	read
back	sorry

Building Future Vocabulary

* These vocabulary words do not appear in this text. They are provided to develop related oral vocabulary that first appears in future texts.

Words:	*light*	*keep*	*drop*
Levels:	Turquoise	Orange	Gold

Comprehension Strategy
Sequencing ideas and story events

Fluency Skill
Matching character's voice

Phonics Skill
Initial sounds: letter *g* (g̲et, g̲etting, g̲ot, g̲one)

Reading-Writing Connection
Copying a phrase

Home Connection
Send home one of the Flying Colors Take-Home books for children to share with their families.

Differentiated Instruction
Before reading the text, query children to discover their level of understanding of the comprehension strategy — Sequencing ideas and story events. As you work together, provide additional support to children who show a beginning mastery of the strategy.

Focus on ELL
- Write words that begin with /g/ on the board. Have children underline the letter *g* in each word.

- Have children write their own words that begin with the *g* sound.

T1

Using This Teaching Version

1. Before Reading

2. During Reading

3. Revisiting the Text

4. Assessment

This Teaching Version will assist you in directing children through the process of reading.

1. **Begin with Before Reading** to familiarize children with the book's content. Select the skills and strategies that meet the needs of your children.

2. **Next, go to During Reading** to help children become familiar with the text, and then to read individually on their own.

3. **Then, go back to Revisiting the Text** and select those specific activities that meet children's needs.

4. **Finally, finish with Assessment** to confirm children are ready to move forward to the next text.

1 Before Reading

Building Background

- Write the word *slippers* on the board. Read it aloud. Have children describe slippers and share if they wear slippers. Correct any misinformation.

- Introduce the book by reading the title, talking about the cover illustration, and sharing the overview.

Building Future Vocabulary
Use Interactive Modeling Card: Sentence Maker

- Introduce the word *light*. Ask *What is light?* (brightness, shining) *Where does it come from?* (sun, lightbulbs, fire)

- Have children fill in the top of the Sentence Maker with the word *light*. Ask children to think of phrases and a sentence to complete the chart.

Introduction to Reading Vocabulary

- On blank cards write: *slippers*, *outside*, and *steps*. Read them aloud. Tell children these words will appear in the text of *Fred's Doghouse*.

- Use each word in a sentence for understanding.

Introduction to Comprehension Strategy

- Explain that authors arrange the events of a story in a sequence of beginning, middle, and end.
- Tell children they will be summarizing the beginning, middle, and end of *Fred's Doghouse*.
- Using the illustrations on pages 2 and 3, have children predict what happens first in the story.

Introduction to Phonics

- List on the board: **got**, **gone**. Read the words aloud and use them in sentences. Point out that both words begin with the letter *g*.
- Together come up with a sentence that uses words beginning with *g,* such as *Girls like to go golfing.* Then write the sentence on the board and underline each *g*.
- Have children look for words that begin with *g* as they read *Fred's Doghouse*.

Modeling Fluency

- Read aloud what Rosie says on pages 12 and 14, modeling a loud voice on page 12 and a softer voice on page 14.
- Have children read the pages aloud, matching Rosie's voice. Discuss how a character's emotions indicate how his or her dialogue should be read.

2 During Reading

Book Talk
Beginning on page T4, use the During Reading notes on the left-hand side to engage children in a book talk. On page 16, follow with Individual Reading.

T3

During Reading

Book Talk

- Explain to children that the events in a story are the actions that take place.

- **Comprehension Strategy** Ask *What is the book about?* (Fred trying to get Rosie out of bed)

- Discuss the title page illustration. Encourage children to make predictions about what Fred does in the story.

Turn to page 2 – Book Talk

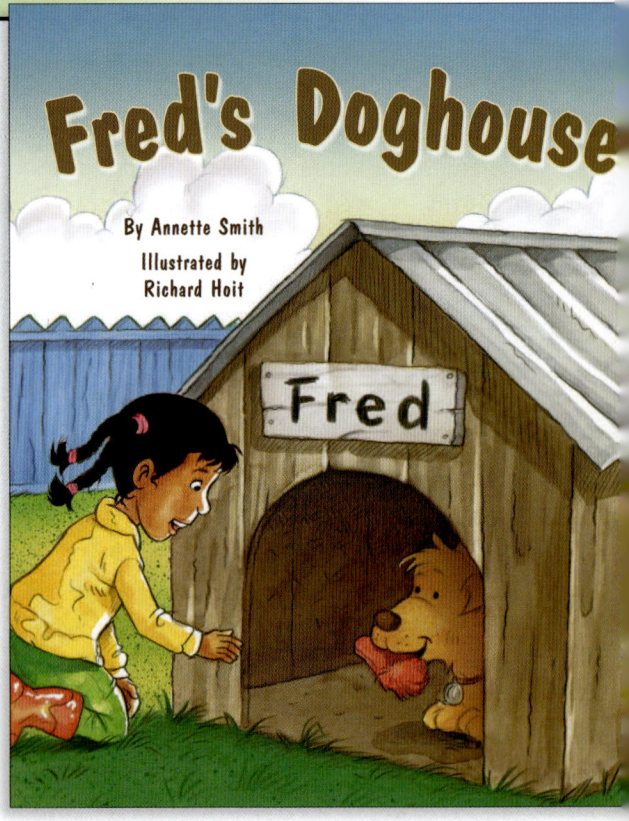

Revisiting the Text

Future Vocabulary
- Look at the cover illustration. Ask *Are there any clues in the cover illustration that tell us the dog will keep something?* (Yes. He has a slipper.)

Now revisit pages 2–3

During Reading

Book Talk

- **Comprehension Strategy** Ask *What is Fred doing?* (barking) *Why do you think he is barking?* (He's trying to get Rosie's attention.) *Can you guess why Fred is trying to get Rosie's attention?* (He's hungry.)
- Ask *Why else might a dog bark?* (fear, pain, happiness)

Turn to page 4 – Book Talk

One day, Rosie said to Fred, "It is too cold to get out of bed this morning. I want to stay here all day."

Revisiting the Text

Rosie got some of her best books. She put the blanket around her, and she started to read.

Future Vocabulary

- Ask *Is there a light in this picture?* (yes, by the bed) *Why does Rosie have her light on?* (to see what she is reading) *Do you have a light in your room?*

- Explain the phrase "drop everything" to children. Discuss with children why Fred wants Rosie to drop everything and follow him.

Now revisit pages 4–5

During Reading

Book Talk

- Have children locate the word *getting* on this page and point out the initial *g*. Brainstorm other words that begin with /g/ and write them on the board.

- **Fluency Skill** Ask *Do you think Fred is barking loudly? Why?* (yes; exclamation points, spiky speech bubbles) Have children model the sound Fred is making.

Turn to page 6 — Book Talk

"Do you want your breakfast?"
Rosie said to Fred.
"I'm sorry,
but you will have to wait.
I'm not getting out of bed yet."

4

Revisiting the Text

Fred pulled the blanket.
He pulled and he pulled.
Rosie pulled the blanket, too.

Future Vocabulary
- Ask *What is Rosie trying to keep in this illustration?* (her blanket) *What is Fred doing to keep Rosie from staying in bed?* (barking and trying to take her blanket) *Why does Fred keep trying to get Rosie out of bed?* (He wants to eat.)

Now revisit pages 6–7

During Reading

Book Talk

- **Comprehension Strategy** Ask *What is Fred doing now?* (He is looking at Rosie's slippers.) *What do you think will happen next?* (Fred will take the slippers.)

- Ask *Why do you think we call that kind of shoe a slipper?* (because we slip them onto our feet)

Turn to page 8 – Book Talk

Rosie laughed,
"You can't pull
the blanket off me today, Fred."

Fred looked at Rosie.
Then he looked at her slippers.
They were on the floor
by her bed.

Revisiting the Text

Future Vocabulary
- Ask *What does Rosie keep in this picture?* (her blanket) *If Rosie stays in bed, what will she keep Fred from doing?* (eating)

Now revisit pages 8–9

During Reading

Book Talk

- **Comprehension Strategy** Ask *What is happening on these pages?* (Rosie is yelling at Fred, and Fred is running away with the slipper.) *Why is Fred doing this?* (to get Rosie to follow him)

- **Fluency Skill** Read aloud Rosie's dialogue, first in a soft voice and then in a loud voice. Ask *Which voice better matches how Rosie is speaking?* (loud voice) *Why?* (The exclamation points show that Rosie is yelling because she is angry with Fred.)

Turn to page 10 – Book Talk

Fred got one of Rosie's slippers. He started to run away with it. He ran out of the room.

Revisiting the Text

Future Vocabulary
- Say *Fred takes Rosie's slipper. Do you think Fred will drop it?* (no) *Why not?* (He wants Rosie to follow him. He wants her to get him something to eat.)

Now revisit pages 10–11

During Reading

Book Talk

- **Comprehension Strategy** Ask *What is happening on these pages?* (Rosie is chasing after Fred.) *Were your predictions correct?*

- Have children locate a word that begins with /g/. *(gone)* Remind them of the other words beginning with *g* that they came up with earlier in the lesson.

Turn to page 12 – Book Talk

Rosie jumped out of bed.
She ran to find Fred.
Where **was** he?

Revisiting the Text

Someone had left the back door open, and Fred had gone outside. He had gone outside with Rosie's slipper.

Future Vocabulary
- Ask *What does Fred plan to keep away from Rosie in this picture?* (her slipper) *What types of things do people try to keep away from dogs?* (valuable things, jewelry, rugs, clothes, shoes)

Now revisit pages 12–13

During Reading

Book Talk

- **Comprehension Strategy** Ask *What does Rosie do first?* (She puts on her jacket.) *What does she do next?* (She puts on her boots.) *What does Rosie do last?* (She runs down the steps.)

- Ask *What does the picture show Rosie doing?* (She is yelling.)

- **Fluency Skill** Have a volunteer read the last two lines on page 12, modeling a yelling voice.

Turn to page 14 – Book Talk

Rosie put on her jacket, and she put on her boots.

She ran down the steps and into the yard.

"Fred! **Fred!**" shouted Rosie. "Where are you?"

Revisiting the Text

Then she saw him.

Fred was hiding in his doghouse.

Future Vocabulary

- Ask *How does this illustration show that it is light outside?* (blue sky, shadows on the ground)

- Say *Light can also mean "not heavy." Do you think Rosie's slipper is light or heavy?* (light)

Now revisit pages 14–15

During Reading

Book Talk

- **Comprehension Strategy**
  Ask *What is happening on these pages?* (Rosie is talking to Fred and trying to get her slipper.)

- **Phonics Skill** Have children locate the words that begin with *g* on these pages. *(get, go)*

Turn to page 16 – Book Talk

"I can see you, Fred," said Rosie. "Come out with my slipper."

But Fred did not come out. Rosie looked inside the doghouse. She could see her slipper.

Revisiting the Text

She tried to get it,
but Fred would not let it go.

"I'm coming to get my slipper," she said. "You can't trick me!"

Future Vocabulary
- Ask *Why does Fred refuse to drop Rosie's slipper?* (He wants Rosie to feed him.)
- Discuss with children whether Fred's plan to keep Rosie's slipper worked.

Go to page T5 – Revisiting the Text

During Reading

Book Talk
- Leave this page for children to discover on their own when they read the book individually.

Individual Reading
Have each child read the entire book at his or her own pace while remaining in the group.

Go to page T5 – Revisiting the Text

The slipper fell out of Fred's mouth.

"Thank you, Fred," laughed Rosie. "Now I will get your breakfast."

Rosie and Fred ran up the steps and into the house.

16

During independent work time, children can read the online book at:
www.rigbyflyingcolors.com

16

Revisiting the Text

Future Vocabulary
- Use the notes on the right-hand pages to develop oral vocabulary that goes beyond the text. These vocabulary words first appear in future texts. These words are: *light*, *keep*, and *drop*.

Turn back to page 1

Reading Vocabulary Review
Activity Sheet: Word Map

- Have children write the word *outside* in the Word Map diamond.
- Have children complete the Word Map with descriptive words and phrases and examples of things that are *outside*.

Comprehension Strategy Review
Use Interactive Modeling Card: Summarizing

- Discuss *Fred's Doghouse.* Together fill in the Summarizing chart.
- Refer to the text and use the discussion questions on page T7 to review story events with children.

Phonics Review
- Have children look for words with initial *g*. (*get:* pp. 2, 15, 16; *got:* pp. 3, 8; *gone:* p. 11)
- Review the list of words that begin with /g/ that children brainstormed earlier. Have children write one or two sentences using words from the list.

Fluency Review
- Partner children and have them take turns reading Rosie's dialogue.
- Remind them to read sentences using an appropriate voice, such as speaking loudly when Rosie is yelling. Talk about how matching Rosie's voice helps them better understand her feelings.

Reading-Writing Connection
Activity Sheet: Character Profile

To assist children with linking reading and writing:
- Have children use the Character Profile to describe Rosie or Fred.
- Have children copy phrases from the story to fill in details.

T5

4 Assessment

Assessing Future Vocabulary

Work with each child individually. Ask questions that elicit each child's understanding of the Future Vocabulary words. Note each child's responses:

- When would you need to use a light? What time of day do you turn on your lights?
- What things do you keep in your backpack or cubby?
- Name some things you might drop into a trash can.

Assessing Comprehension Strategy

Work with each child individually. Note each child's understanding of sequencing ideas and story events:

- Where did this story take place?
- What was the first thing that happened in *Fred's Doghouse*?
- What happened next?
- What happened last in the story?
- Was each child able to tell you what happened at the beginning, middle, and end of the story?

Assessing Phonics

Work with each child individually. Have each child write words from the story that begin with /g/. Note each child's responses for understanding initial *g*:

- Use the following words: *go, gas,* and *game.*
- Did each child understand that only the first letter should be the letter *g*?
- Did each child pronounce the words correctly?

Assessing Fluency

Have each child read pages 9 and 16 to you. Note each child's understanding of matching the character's voice:

- Did each child use a loud voice on page 9?
- Did each child use a low voice on page 16?
- Did each child understand the different emotions Rosie was feeling on each page?

Interactive Modeling Cards

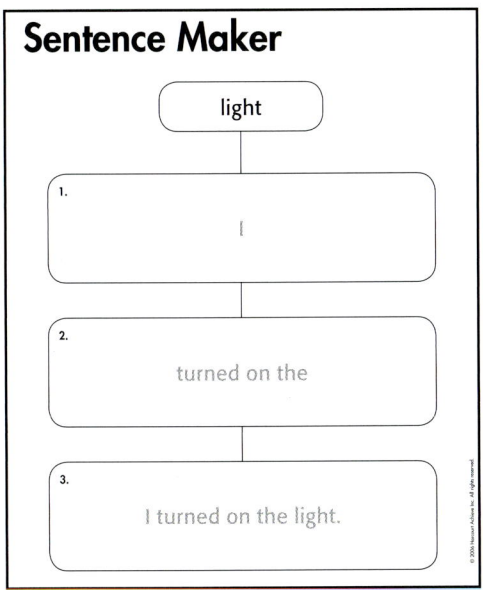

Directions: With children, fill in the Sentence Maker using the word *light*.

Summarizing

Page	Summary
2–3	Rosie wants to stay in bed.
4–7	Fred wants his breakfast, so he tries to get Rosie out of bed.
8–15	Fred steals Rosie's slipper so she has to get out of bed.
16	Rosie agrees to feed Fred.

Directions: With children, fill in the Summarizing chart for *Fred's Doghouse*.

Discussion Questions

- What was the main event in the story? (Literal)
- What were the problems in this book? How were they solved? (Critical Thinking)
- How do you think Fred felt when Rosie would not get out of bed? (Inferential)

T7

Activity Sheets

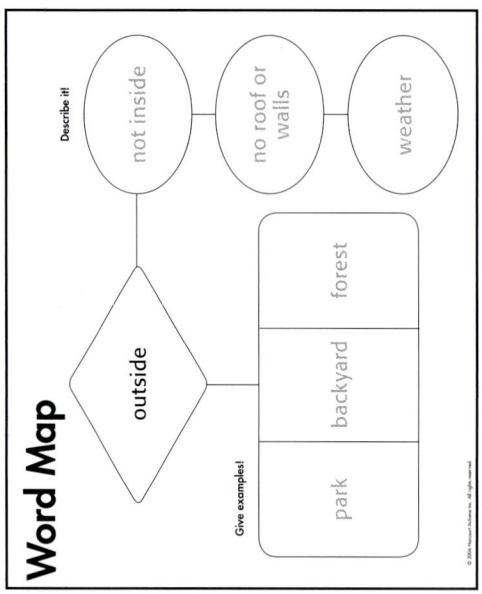 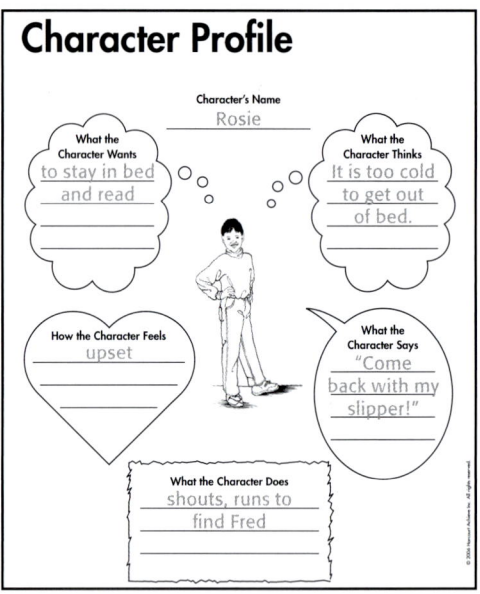

Directions: Have children fill in the Word Map using the word *outside*.

Directions: Have children, independently or with a partner, fill in the Character Profile for Rosie or Fred. Have them copy phrases from the book to fill in details.